RAREBITS
For Welsh Learners

BY COLIN JONES

CADW sŵn

Rarebits for Welsh Learners

By Colin Jones

Published by Cadw Sŵn

www.cadwswn.com

Hawlfraint © Copyright Cadw Sŵn MMXVIII

All rights reserved worldwide.

Rarebits for Welsh Learners

Colin Jones

CADW sŵn

CONTENTS

Introduction 1

Welsh is a spoken language 4

The soft mutation 6

Magu Clust 12

Idioms – 1 14

    Mae e'n cadw draenog yn ei boced 14

    Gwell hwyr na hwyrach 14

The Curious Case of the Shorter Plurals 15

More Plurals 20

Idioms – 2 21

    Cer i grafu 21

    Dilyn 'sgwarnog 21

Croesi'r Bont 22

Flexible thinking and improving your mind 25

A Welsh Flipper 28

Idioms – 3 31

Sit down, stand up 32

The Nasal Mutation 33

Why do we soften questions and negatives? 35

The Easiest Tense on the Planet - 1 39

The Easiest Tense on the Planet - 2 40

Idioms - 4 43

    Diwedd y gan yw'r geiniog 43

    Siarad fel melin bupur 43

Why is there no 'it' in Welsh? 44

The Old Numbers 47
Yn and Mewn – In 49
Idioms - 5 50
    Dros Ben Llestri 50
    Malu awyr 50
'Mynd at' and 'Mynd i' 51
The Long and Winding Road 52
The Final Mutation 55
The Short Form Past of Bod 56
Idioms - 6 59
    Gwell crefft na golud 59
    Breuddwyd gwrach 59
The Secret to Learning Welsh 60
Cnoc, Cnoc! 62
The Cadw Swn Guide to Speaking Welsh 63
The Myth of 'Difficult' Languages 64
The magical first-language Welsh speaker 66
Idiots Guide 68
The Secret to Siarad Cymraeg 70
All the Tenses you Could Ever Need 73

INTRODUCTION

One of the things that I do to scrape a meagre living is teach Welsh to adults, both through books and in Welsh classes. I often find that I have certain ways of explaining some things in class which are mildly entertaining and sometimes even useful. I've been thinking that if I were to get run over by a bus, or (less likely) to retire, these little monologues would disappear forever.

Things should not disappear forever, and I think I can see a large red vehicle on the horizon, so this might be my best chance to write these little gems down. You never know.

This book is a collection of those times when I feel myself 'going off on one' to launch into one of my five-minute explanations in class. I sometimes think that I enjoy these more than the class does, but I do think that they're useful and I hope you will too. I've been a Welsh-to-adults tutor for longer than I care to remember (actually over 20 years) and this book is filled with things that I've taken time to mull over and try to explain in a clear and entertaining way. I've had the luxury, like a stand-up comedian, of being able to try things out in class, see what works, and see what falls as flat as a pancake run over by a steamroller.

You'll find such things as 'why are things either male or female in Welsh', 'why are some plural words shorter than the singular' and so on. The explanations which I give may or may not be

Colin Jones

100% correct, but they are hopefully memorable and of use. You'll also find a selection of my favourite idioms, jokes, and a few cartoons along the way, many featuring the Rarebits, a strange band of little-seen cheese-eating rabbits. Possibly.

I hope you'll dip into the book at various points in your learning, or even read it through from start to finish. It can usually pay to take stock, have a rethink, listen to another person's point of view. This book aims to be just another piece of the jigsaw on the road to Welsh fluency. Pob lwc!

THE (MANY) STAGES OF LEARNING

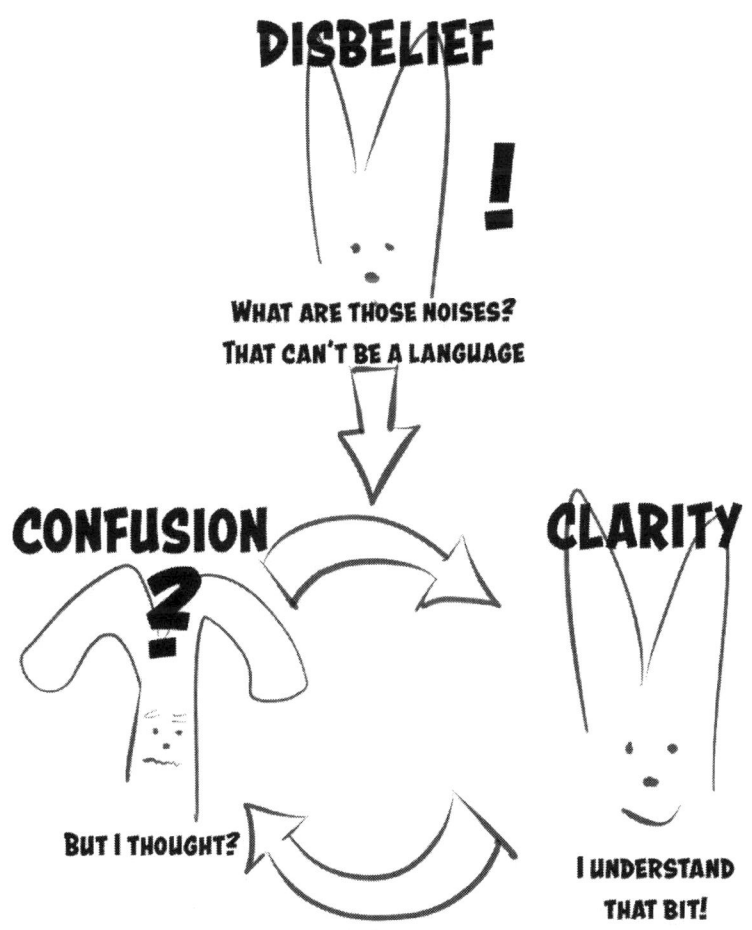

DISBELIEF

!

WHAT ARE THOSE NOISES?
THAT CAN'T BE A LANGUAGE

CONFUSION

?

BUT I THOUGHT?

CLARITY

I UNDERSTAND THAT BIT!

THIS GOES ON FOR QUITE A WHILE UNTIL...

HAPPINESS

I'VE GOT IT!

Colin Jones

WELSH IS A SPOKEN LANGUAGE

I cannot over-emphasise how important this is. Welsh is an old language, an ancient language; one of Europe's oldest living languages. It had been spoken for thousands of years before anyone could write down a single word of it. The idea of a written, stable language had not yet evolved, at least in Britain. The rules, tenses, mutations and general structure are a lot easier to grasp as sounds, or patterns, or as speech. Simply put, Welsh can seem a lot more difficult when it's written down. Actually, Welsh can be more than a little difficult when it's written down, and often simpler when we hear it, or speak it as sounds.

The way that Welsh works is tied up in its oral roots, and quite often I find that if something seems difficult it's often worth saying it aloud and listening to the sounds.

The ancient Britons had no qualms about changing the tone of spoken words, matter of fact we still do this to day – 'I did *what* last night in the pub?' is a phrase which springs to mind. We're also quite happy to put a sing-song chime into words and phrases – 'Hon-ey, I'm ho-ome!', and why not? It adds character and lets us be a little playful with our languages.

Likewise, to Welsh-speakers there's no shame in altering the actual words themselves; why shouldn't 'cath' become 'gath' or even 'chath' if it seems right? Before words became written down, quite literally etched in stone, nobody had told us that we couldn't muck around with them. So we did, and still do to this day. Take the Soft Mutation, for instance (no, please; take the soft mutation)...

Colin Jones

THE SOFT MUTATION

Ah, the soft mutation. If you see this written down you might like to run a mile (I often like to run a mile, my doctor tells me it keeps my blood pressure down). However, and here's the beauty of reading a book in the correct sequence, if you've read the previous page you may have an idea of what's coming; the mutations can be moderately easy if you forget about the written word and listen to the sounds. It's all to do with patterns...

Patterns

Welsh is just a series of sound patterns. The strength of patterns is that if something breaks a pattern we notice immediately. That makes them memorable. Take a look at the following pattern, and where the pattern is broken. Notice how your eye is drawn to where the pattern is broken;

As soon as a pattern is broken it becomes obvious. Similarly, if someone is singing the wrong note we'll most likely hear it. Welsh is a series of sound patterns. Once you get used to these patterns it becomes more difficult to get things wrong. Things really do start to fall into place.

The only way to learn the mutations is to say them. Never use the names of letters; 'ay', 'bee', 'see' etc, always use the sounds that they form; 'ah', 'buh', etc. Then just begin to notice the way that your mouth changes these sounds to mutate them.

Take the place-name Tondu. The easy way of learning to 'do' the soft mutation is to say the words aloud, and notice how you make the sounds. Prepare yourself for some puzzled stares if you're in company, but if you say 'Tondu' aloud,

'Tondu' Then

'o Dondu' (from Tondu)

'tuh' (the sound that the letter T makes)

'duh' (the sound that the letter D makes)

And if you can bring yourself to repeat 'tuh' and 'duh' a few dozen times, while noticing just how you form the sounds in your mouth, and how the other people on the bus react.

Notice that the two sounds are made in a very similar way in your mouth, and that you could almost think that you're processing the same sound 'tuh' in some subtle way to make the 'duh' sound. It's almost as if you're rounding the sound off or (ahem) *softening* it in some way, just by using your mouth slightly differently. If that makes any kind of sense you're pretty much covered on the basics of the soft mutation. If it makes no sense at all have another go at the above few paragraphs.

Tuh – duh

TA-DA!

Now all that's needed is to go through the other 8 letters (only 9 can ever mutate) and be a little curious, observing how your mouth forms these letters. Then you can begin to see that you're doing the same thing to all of them to process, or mutate, the sounds.

I'd have called it 'processing' rather than 'mutating' but then what do I know?

ARGH! IT'S A MUTATION!

NO DEAR, IT'S JUST A PROCESS!

'Cuh' (the sound that the letter c makes in cornet and caravan)

'Guh' (the sound the letter 'g' makes in gloom and Granny Smith)

'Puh' – 'Buh'

Now carry on aloud with the following, making the sounds of the letters rather than the names. Repeat as often as you can.

'B' - 'F'

'G' - ' ' (disappears)

'Rh' - 'R'

Colin Jones

'M' - 'F'

'Ll' - 'L'

In the future you'll need to know when to use the soft mutation, of course, but for now it'll be enough just to understand and accept it; notice it when it happens and be reasonably happy that it's there.

If you ever get stuck, and are really keen to find out what a letter mutates to, a simple trick is to think of a place name starting with that letter and to say you're from that place.

Tondu - Dw i'n dod o Dondu. (I come from Tondu)

The 'o' (when it means 'from', not just the letter 'o') causes the next word to soften. Here are some more place names for you to read aloud, especially if you're still on that bus.

Tondu - o Dondu

Caerdydd - o Gaerdydd

Penybont - o Benybont

Bangor - o Fangor

Gwaelod y Garth - o Waelod y Garth

Dolgellau - o Ddolgellau

Rhydaman - o Rydaman

Maesteg - o Faesteg

Llangynwyd - o Langynwyd

Rarebits for Welsh Learners

To recap nine letters change as follows. Try to say the sounds of the letters rather than the names and you'll be fine.

T - D

C - G

P - B

B - F

G - * (disappears)

D - Dd

Rh - R

M - F

Ll - L

MAGU CLUST

Magu is to bring up, or to raise (as in to raise a child). Clust is an ear. Magu clust is a phrase we use to convey the idea of just hearing what sounds right in Welsh so that you can speak naturally and easily.

I like to think of magu clust as Maggie Clust, a famous opera singer who can break pint glasses simply by finding the correct note to blast out in the pub. Don't mess with Maggie, or she'll have you weeping over your lost pint.

Have you ever noticed someone saying tom-aye-toe in the UK instead of tom-ar-to? That's your ear telling you that something's amiss. If you had been brought up in the US you'd be perfectly happy with 'tom-aye-toe' because that's what everyone around you would say.

That's all we do in Welsh; we say what everyone else does. Since we hear mostly correct Welsh we'll say mostly correct Welsh. It really is as simple as that.

IDIOMS – 1

Mae e'n cadw draenog yn ei boced

He keeps a hedgehog in his pocket. A person who finds it difficult, even painful to spend money. A miser.

Gwell hwyr na hwyrach
Better late than later. I use this in my classes all the time, as people stroll in just before coffee. I do mean it, though. Very similar to the English 'better late than never'.

THE CURIOUS CASE OF THE SHORTER PLURALS

Plurals in English are pretty simple, right? I mean, we just need to add an 's' to the word. House, houses. Mouse, erm, mice. Oh well. Anyhow, singular words in English are pretty much always shorter than the plural. That's not always the case in Welsh.

Not to worry, it'll all become perfectly clear if you read on…

Amser maith yn ôl – a long long ago, ancient Celtic man and woman were standing on a hill at midnight. They were at the beginnings of language, and were making up sounds for things. They looked into the sky, the clouds cleared, and they saw – stars. Yes, a clear, glowing host of stars – sêr.

Sêr – stars. It was the group that they noticed first, so it was perfectly natural that the word they created was for the plural. Then, after a while, they began to notice that one of the stars – *sêr un*, was a little brighter than the rest. After even more time, they began to think that maybe you could use this star – *sêr un* – to find your way around the countryside. This *sêr-un* became *seren* through repetition across many generations.

Sêr – stars

Seren – a star (one of the stars)

And so the ancient pair of bardic name-makers went down into the valley. They noticed the trees ahead – coed.

It was becoming quite cold by now, and they were eager to start a fire for warmth. Amongst the coed (trees) one small sapling *coed-un* (one of the trees) was ripe for felling. The tree – *coed un* – burnt well, and they began their search for food.

Coed – trees

Coeden – a tree

In a clearing some wild pigs were foraging. 'Moch!' screamed one of the pair - look, there are pigs. The pigs – moch – were unaware of the ancient hunters. One of the pigs – *moch un* – was a little slower than the others, and this *moch-un* became a hearty feast for the duo.

Moch – pigs

Mochyn – a pig (moch-un over time became mochyn)

Colin Jones

The next morning the pair noticed a flock of birds – adar – flying overhead. The birds seemed to be on a journey southwards, but the pair noticed that one bird – *adar un* – was injured and unlikely to complete the journey.

Adar – birds

Aderyn – a bird (adar-un over a long period of time)

It seemed obvious to the pair to form words in this way, in each case it was the plural which caught their attention first, followed by the singular.

There are many other examples, including the following

Plant – children

Plentyn – a child

Dail – leaves

Deilen – a leaf

Selsig – sausages (always best and always bought in the plural)

Selsigen – a sausage

Madarch – mushrooms

Madarchen – a mushroom

The list goes on with many more examples. However, you never need to worry which is the singular and which is the plural of these words. If the last syllable seems like it could have come from 'un' the Welsh for one, then that is almost certainly the singular.

It also seems to make sense in that all these words are usually first seen in the plural, with the singular following at a later point. You'll find other words, lots of fruits for instance, follow this pattern.

MORE PLURALS

Castell - a castle

Cestyll - castles

Menig - a glove

Maneg - Gloves

Cerrig - a stone

Carreg - stones

Notice the way the first syllables of these words change; from 'a' in the singular to 'e' in the plural. That's your key to remembering which is the singular and which is the plural. Once you have one pair of words committed to memory the others should always be there. Say them aloud a few times until you begin to commit the pattern to memory.

IDIOMS – 2

Cer i grafu

Go and scratch – get lost. I seem to remember that this originally came from the phrase 'go and scratch your stomach with your toenails' but that might just have been a bad dream.

Dilyn 'sgwarnog

To follow a hare. To go off on a tangent. There I was, walking along a leafy path when a hare jumped across my path. I got distracted and followed the hair, leaving the path. I went off at a tangent.

It's both one of my favourite Welsh idioms and pastimes.

CROESI'R BONT

'Croesi'r Bont' is a phrase that is often used to describe the journey of a Welsh learner. It contains a good few truths and some interesting insights into learning Welsh.

Here's a simple bridge. It's based on Yr Hen Bont – the old bridge in Penybont. Dw i'n dod o Benybont yn wreiddiol, you know. I've said it now.

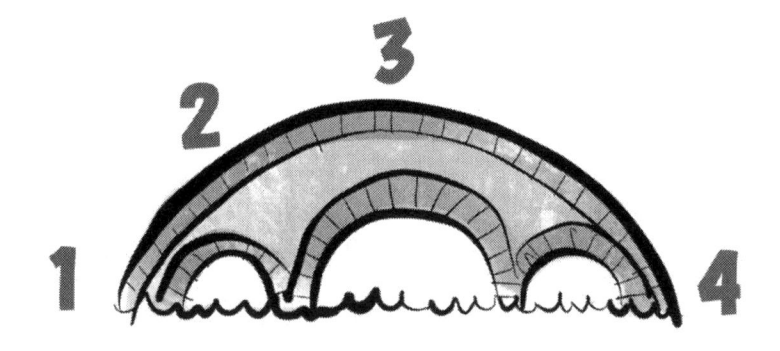

If you imagine that a Welsh learner is standing to the left of the bridge at point 1 you can notice a number of things.

Firstly, she can't see over the bridge – there might not be anyone or anything on the other side. So learning Welsh is an act of trust; we're pretty sure that there are Welsh speakers, but until we actually start a conversation in Welsh we can't really be sure that it's not all an elaborate hoax. Secondly, once she begins learning the initial slope of the bridge is very steep. Everything is new, the sounds, spellings, mutations, etc. This would be the point where many people give up, simply because it's the most difficult point of the journey. The learning curve is at its steepest.

You've gone beyond the very first step, of actually beginning to learn Welsh, by beginning to read this book. You now know something about Welsh, even if this is your very first experience of the language, so Welsh can never be as difficult again. Think of that for an instant; Welsh can never be quite as difficult again. Ah.

You can then begin to move slowly upwards over the first part of the bridge. Notice that the learning curve, or the slope of the bridge, begins to get a little less steep. You might not notice this at the time, since you're still being bombarded with new vocabulary and tenses, but Welsh is getting easier. From point 1 to 2 on the bridge it's still an effort, but your time learning and practicing begins to pay off, maybe at this point you can even start to enjoy the journey.

At point 3 you're half way over the bridge, and there are a couple of things to notice; firstly, you can see the other side of the bridge. Look, there are actually people over there, speaking Welsh, laughing, arguing, singing, having fun and being miserable. All through the medium of Welsh. That might spur you on, you might even begin to hear them.

But there's another thing to note; at the mid-point of the bridge the learning curve stops sloping upwards. From this point another interesting thing can happen, if you let it; unless you physically stop yourself gravity begins to take effect. That's a wonderful thing, your natural place of rest is now actually on the other side of the bridge.

You could, of course, stop yourself and turn back. You could even jump off the bridge, but why would you? As long as you can remember that you're on this mildly interesting journey you could instead give yourself a pat on the back and carry on, with a smile and a whistle to the other side.

Then you'll have two languages, two windows on the world, two ways of thinking. And it gets even more interesting than that…

FLEXIBLE THINKING AND IMPROVING YOUR MIND

Learning another language as an adult is one of the best things you can do to keep your mind flexible and active. Research is continually telling us that learning another language as an adult can help our resistance to many conditions associated with our minds and aging.

Here's one thing I've noticed which might help us understand some of the changes that are happening. Once you start on your language learning adventure you begin to notice the way you think changing somewhat, sometimes quite early on your journey. I often use this example in class…

Maybe you're driving or walking to a Welsh class. You might pass a library, or a school, or some other public building. If it's a school for instance, you'll start out by noticing the school and thinking nothing more of it.

SCHOOL   **SCHOOL**

After a few weeks of learning Welsh though, you might say to yourself 'ah, the Welsh for school is Ysgol' or 'ah, the Welsh for library is llyfrgell' as your mind begins translating.

SCHOOL   **YSGOL**

A month or so later and something remarkable begins to happen. At one point, since you're on your way to Welsh class you might be in 'Welsh mode' and your mind might go straight to 'ysgol' or 'llyfrgell' when you see the building without translating from the English. Of course you don't lose the ability to think in English, so if you're in 'English-speaking mode' you'll go straight to 'school' or 'library'. You'll then have two ways of thinking, two pathways.

SCHOOL

YSGOL

Notice that the original translation path from 'school' to 'ysgol' is no longer used. And what happens to a pathway in a field that's no longer used? It grows over, and disappears back into the field. When you're learning a language you must get thousands of such changes in your mind, not just with vocabulary but tenses too. You can begin to imagine the incredible changes for the good which are going on in your mind. Your mind becomes more flexible, which can have knock-on effects in other areas. All these new pathways and patterns are being formed, and old ones healing over.

Colin Jones

A WELSH FLIPPER

Now this is something really special. I kid you not.

The following two pages may well be worth the price of this book alone. Simply tear out the page, cut along the dotted lines, and fold along the solid black lines.

Then, like a mad uncle at a drunken party, you should get ready to amaze your friends and work colleagues with your incredible display of Welsh dexterity.

"Ah, but I'm listening to the audio book version", you might say (but strangely in my own voice) or "I don't want to destroy this beautiful work of art", or even "Hang on a flippin' minute, this is an ebook, how on earth am I supposed to tear the flippin' pages of this flippin' flipper out!?!"

Do not worry dear reader, simply go to www.cadwswn.com/flipper and marvel at a spectacular pdf to print out at your leisure. Feel free to pass the delightful pdf on to friends, relations or random strangers. Remember to tell them where you got it, of course, and about how this mildly interesting book spurred you on to greater heights of Welsh fluency and acrobatics. Fold the flaps over to make sentences. Take one box from the top, one from the middle, and one from the bottom. Eg. Dw i + 'n + bwyta - Dw i'n bwyta.

By the way, 'a page' in Welsh is 'tudalen' while a leaf (two pages) is 'deilen'. Just like in English a page is one of those funny things that can't actually exist on its own. It always needs a butty.

**Cut along the dotted lines, then fold along the black lines.
How many sentences can you make?**

Maen nhw (they)	Dw i (I)	Dyn ni (we)
'n mynd i (going to)	'n (Am/are/is)	wedi (have/has)
yfed	bwyta	cerdded

| Rwyt ti
You (familiar) | Dych chi
You (formal) | Mae e
Mae hi
He/she |
| wedi
have/has | 'n
Am/are/is | 'n mynd i
going to |
| cogionio | edrych ar y teledu | chwarae |

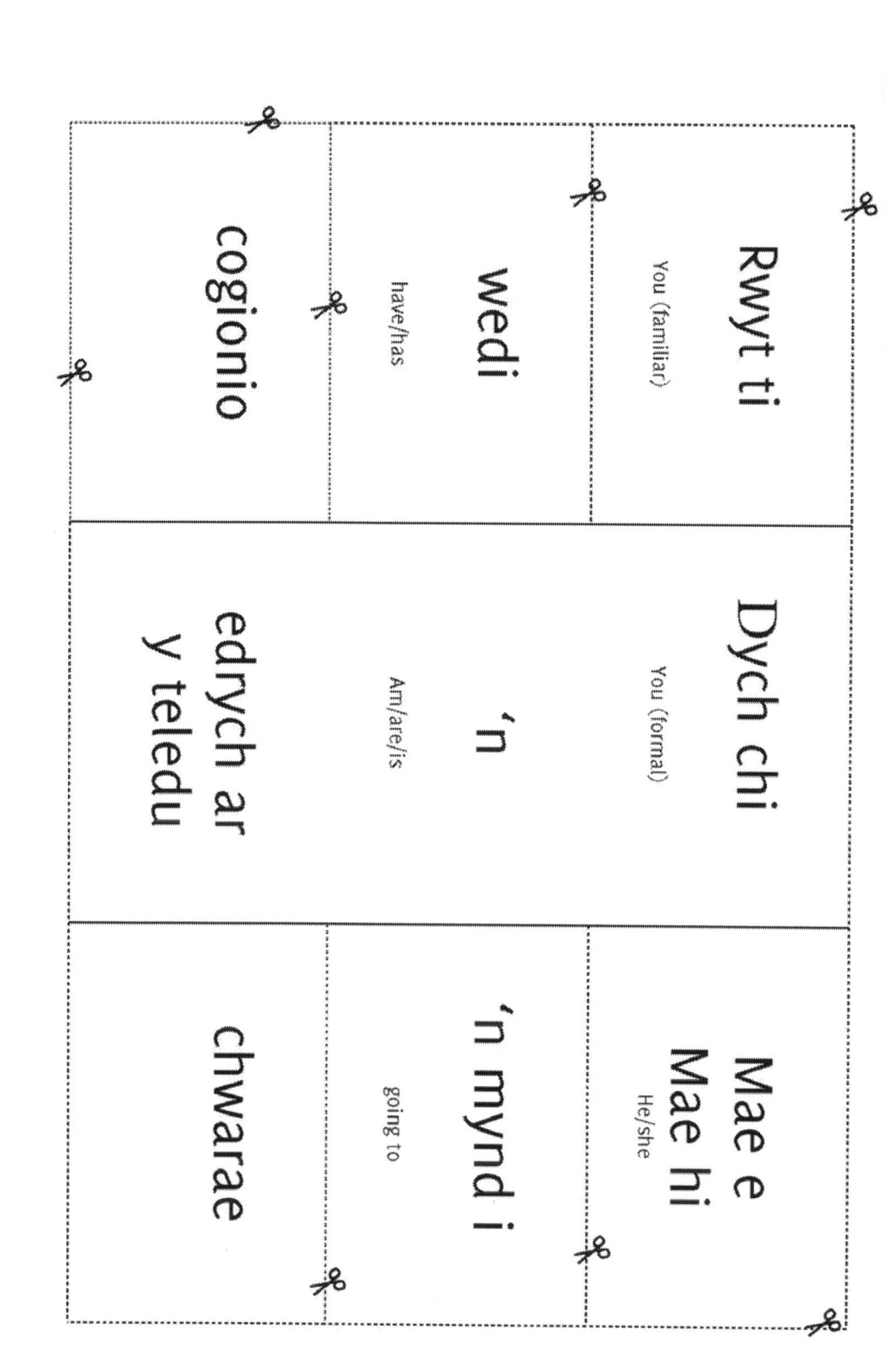

IDIOMS – 3

Agor y tap – to turn the tap on (open the tap)

Cau'r tap – to turn the tap off (close the tap)

Makes sense, I'm sure you'll agree, and always nicer to use phrases which are more natural in Welsh.

Wedi suro – has soured (gone off).

Mae'r llaeth wedi suro. The milk has gone off.

Teachers and tutors love this sort of malarkey. 'Miss, my pen's run out.', says poor little Elwyn, eager to finish his essay on interesting Welsh existentialist authors. 'Well run out after it, then!' Miss answers, chuckling wildly to herself.

SIT DOWN, STAND UP

There are a number of words in Welsh which take extra elements in English. Here are a few examples where we don't need to add a direction in Welsh;

Ysgrifennu – to write down

Eistedd – to sit down

Sefyll – to stand up

Pwyllo – to calm down

You might need to add extra words in Welsh for some phrases (stand down, sit up) but the basic verbs are enough for the default use.

THE NASAL MUTATION

This sound-shift, perhaps even more than the Soft Mutation, only really works in speech. On paper, it's almost impossible to remember, but once you get used to the way of processing the sound it'll become second nature.

I always tell my pupils that I cannot remember the nasal mutation, but I can always get it right, which is true. What I mean is that I can 'do' the mutation in speech, without thinking. So if someone in a class asks 'what does p change to in the nasal mutation' I always go through the following motions;

I walk slowly but purposefully to the board, then as I write I say to myself 'Penybont – Ym Mhenybont'. I copy the mutated letter which I hear to the board. As a tutor I feel I should know which letters mutate, which is in fact the difficult bit. I remember one of my pupils saying 'TCP, bloody good disinfectant' which they learnt from another tutor.

So that's the difficult bit

Then I write 't,c,p,b,g,d' and go through the process with place names, saying 'yn' followed by the place name in my head as I copy the correct letters from my mind's ear.

Tondu, yn Nhondu

Caerdydd – yng Nghaerdydd

Penybont, ym Mhenybont

Colin Jones

Bangor – ym Mangor

Gwynedd – yng Ngwynedd

Dolgellau – yn Nolgellau

You should approach the nasal mutation the same way as the soft mutation; just read the above aloud, being conscious of how you make the sounds and how those sounds are processed (mutated) for the nasal mutation. I'd strongly suggest that you never rely on those tables often found in grammar books which list the letters and their mutations. However, if you do, always read the sounds of the letters (tu, cuh, etc) rather than the names of the letters (tee, cee, etc).

Oh yes. When do we use the nasal mutation? After 'yn' meaning 'in' and 'fy' meaning 'my'. Probably a few other times too, but as they say that's beyond the scope of this book. Ha.

WHY DO WE SOFTEN QUESTIONS AND NEGATIVES?

When I was learning Welsh I sometimes listened to the tutor. Not always, and not particularly often, but I do remember the odd occasion. The funny thing is that the very time I listened something would make me a little perplexed. It's odd, the things you remember from tutors and teachers.

Back in school I remember one of the few rules I learnt in English – "I' before 'e' except after 'c". I can never get this to work – the word 'their' springs to mind, but there are dozens of others including eight, weird, weighs, sleigh, etc. I could go on, but you can always search the internet. And you've not come here to have your English grammar put under the microscope, have you?

Anyhow, I remember one tutor telling me that the soft mutation was always caused by a preceding word or pattern; there was always something before the mutation which caused it. But hang on, I thought in one particularly confused state of mind, how come we soften the start of questions, and sometimes negative statements? Then one day one of my pupils told me. I get that a lot.

Have you ever noticed how Spanish often puts an upside-down question mark or exclamation mark at the start of a sentence? This is brilliant for brands and logos as it adds a punchy element to the logo. If there's an upside-down exclamation mark at the start it means that what follows should be exclaimed, if there's an upside-down question mark at the start it means that what follows is a question.

That makes it a lot easier to read passages aloud. I've lost count of the number of times I've started reading a sentence aloud in class, only to find that I should have exclaimed it or made it sound like a question before I get to the end of the sentence and find an exclamation mark or question mark.

These upside-down punctuation marks don't actually mean anything, they're just markers. In this case they tell us that what follows should be exclaimed or said in a questioning tone. Welsh has something quite similar, which explains the softening of questions.

If you're familiar with your Welsh-language nursery rhymes you'll have come across the following;

Mi welais Jac y Do

Yn eistedd ar ben tô

Het wen ar ei ben a dwy goes bren

Ho ho ho ho ho ho

Take a look at the first line –

Mi welais Jac y Do.

I saw a Jackdaw

'Jac y Do' is a Jackdaw.

'Gwelais i' – 'I saw'

But what does the 'mi' mean? It doesn't mean anything; it's a marker. It tells us that what comes next is a statement. It's like the upside-down punctuation marks in Spanish.

In south Wales we might say Fe welais instead of Mi welais, but they're both the same thing; positive markers. They tell us that what follows is a statement. You might hear these occasionally in speech, but you'll be more likely to come across them in formal Welsh; in a book or a public speech for instance. Some Welsh speakers will soften the start of statements because of this. We might have lost the marker in speech but some people still keep the mutation.

The Question Marker

If you go to the National Eisteddfod, and you really should, you might be lucky enough to hear some of the ceremonies. At one point a person will hold up a sheathed sword, bring the sword out a little and ask;

'A oes heddwch?' (Is there peace)

The audience will be very keen to see that the sword goes back into the sheath, so they'll all shout 'Heddwch' to help things along. The sword-wielding bard will however ask again, with the same result - 'Heddwch!' which in Welsh means 'Get that flippin' sword back in its sheath, you lunatic.'

Notice that the 'a' at the start of that sentence is the question marker; it tells us that what follows is a question. Now this 'a' causes what follows to soften, so even though in spoken Welsh we don't tend to use the 'a', the mutation is still there.

Likewise 'ni' is the negative marker, which causes a treiglad llais (t,c,p mutation) or a soft mutation.

Ni welais neb. – I didn't see anyone.

THE EASIEST TENSE ON THE PLANET - 1

If you're familiar with your personal pronouns (I, you, he, she etc) then this tense will take you no time at all to learn. It's the past tense of bod, to be. Since we shorten things so much in spoken welsh, all the work is removed by the abbreviations.

Ro'n i	I was
Ro't ti	You were
Roedd e	He was
Roedd hi	She was
Ro'n ni	We were
Ro'ch chi	You were
Ro'n nhw	They were

Notice how in speech you might just as well put 'ro' in front of ti, ni, chi and nhw. You'd get exactly the same sounds. That's what makes it so easy; all the hard work has been shortened out of the tense.

Ro'n i yn y dref neithiwr - I was in town last night.

Ro'n i'n bwyta - I was eating.

THE EASIEST TENSE ON THE PLANET - 2

You remember **ro'n I** (I was) right? I mean we only did it in the last chapter, actually on the previous page. However, if you studied, or were subjected to, Welsh at school you might have come across the unabbreviated version, which is extremely handy for giving us yet another tense, almost without effort. Many of you will remember it, so let's take a look;

Roeddwn i — I was

Roeddet ti — You were

Roedd e — He was

Roedd hi — She was

Roedden ni — We were

Roeddech chi — You were (plural)

Roedden nhw — They were

This longer, unabbreviated form is more formal, and so is better for written Welsh.

Pan oeddwn i'n ifanc roeddwn i'n cerdded i'r ysgol – When I was young I would walk to school.

Notice the 'would'. This is a strange tense. We can use would in the past or the future;

When I was young I would walk to school

If I won the lottery I would move to Spain.

Odd, eh? Now, if we could imagine that 'roedd' was the stem, just like in the short-form verbs gwelais i, etc. We'd have the following endings;

-wn i

-et ti

The third person (e/hi) doesn't seem to have an ending, so let's just put 'ai' in there for no reason other than it's the right ending.

-ai fe/hi

-en ni

-ech chi

-en nhw

Now let's take a verb, say hoffi, and put the stem (hoff) in front of these endings.

Hoffwn i – I would like

Hoffet ti - you would like

Hoffai fe - he would like

Hoffai hi - she would like

Hoffai John - John would like

Colin Jones

Hoffen ni - we would like

Hoffech chi - you would like

Hoffen nhw - they would like

This gives us the conditional tense.

Hoffwn i fyw yn Sbaen – I would like to live in Spain.

Hoffwn i sglodion - I'd like (some) chips.

This might never happen, conditions need to be met for it to become a reality. I'd like to live in Spain, but in order for that to happen certain things need to take place.

There are a few more verbs we can bolt this pattern onto to gain free and easy access to exotic tenses:

Dylwn i – I should

Gallwn i – I could

Talwn i – I would pay

We could go on, but you get the idea.

IDIOMS - 4

Diwedd y gan yw'r geiniog

At the end of the song comes the penny. It all comes down to money in the end. Ask Maggie Clust, she knows. It's not over until she sings, mind.

Siarad fel melin bupur

To talk like a pepper mill. To talk a lot, one feels.

WHY IS THERE NO 'IT' IN WELSH?

Why are things either male or female in Welsh? Why can't they just call everything 'it' and leave it at that?

Once again, you'll have to cast your mind back into the mists of time. To the ancient Celts there was a life-force in everything; there were gods in the rivers, spirits in the trees. Everything was alive, so it was perfectly natural that things were either male or female. The concept of a lifeless 'it' simply didn't exist.

Now, you might wonder how Welsh-speakers manage to negotiate this minefield of linguistic gender. After all, there doesn't seem to be an easy way to know if something is male or female.

You might notice by now that this book is meant to help you learn Welsh. It covers particular topics which I feel I might be able to cast some light on. What I'm going to write now will hopefully clear up this problem, or at least set your mind to rest. Eventually our old friend Maggie Clust will tell us everything we need to know.

If you think about it, a language wouldn't work if you needed to think if a noun was either male or female. It'd slow you down in speech so much that it just wouldn't be viable. All languages need to work on an instinctive level, where you simply communicate without having to think. Otherwise we'd have probably gotten rid of the male and female nouns by now.

When do we actually need to know when a thing is male or female? More than likely, it's to know if we need to soften it after the 'y' (feminine nouns soften after 'y' or 'un', masculine nouns don't). But this is the thing that we will already know. Our ear will tell us, thanks to Maggie Clust.

Take the Welsh name for Bridgend – Penybont. You're almost certainly familiar with the name, but you're probably also familiar with Pontypridd. You've probably been perfectly happy up to now with the 'pont' in Pontypridd and the 'y bont' in Penybont.

Penybont – the head, or end of the bridge – pen y bont

We know by now that 'pont' must be feminine since it softens after the 'y'. But try saying 'pen y pont'. It's difficult because instinctively we know we should say Penybont. We're building up a library of things that just 'sound right' in our mind. One reason we'd need to know if 'pont' was masculine or feminine would be to decide if we need to soften it after 'y'. But that's the very thing we instinctively know, thanks to you-know-who.

We'll then unknowingly build up a pattern in our heads of softening the adjectives which follow a noun if the noun itself softens after 'y';

Y ddinas – the city

Y ddinas fawr ddrwg – the big bad city

Eventually all the work is done subconsciously, which is the only way it could work. I'd say not to worry too much about the

Colin Jones

gender of nouns, but to accept that it'll probably work itself out. And if you get the gender of the odd noun wrong I can assure you that you're not alone.

THE OLD NUMBERS

You're probably aware that we count in tens, hence the decimal system. Our fingers, or digits, have led us to group numbers in tens; twenty thirty, forty, etc.

However, the ancient Celts were a little more dexterous, and they used their toes as well as their fingers. This led to twenty being the base number in the Celtic languages. That meant that we would group numbers in twenties; twenty, forty, sixty and so on. We'd then add the numbers to these base numbers, which was all very fine and dandy.

Time passed, money was made, animals counted and traded, and all was well in the world.

However, in the mid-twentieth century Welsh-medium education discovered a problem. Multiplication and division was particularly unsuited to the old twenty-based system and children, many of whom came from non-Welsh speaking homes, were left at a disadvantage.

So, the decimal system finally came to Wales! Hurray! Street parties were held, holidays taken and celebrations erupted throughout the country. Actually that bit's not true, but it was some sort of a milestone.

It's the decimal system that's widespread today, and you're no doubt familiar with un deg un, un deg dau, etc.

As a matter of fact since the decimal system was developed much later in Wales it has proved easier for Welsh-medium pupils since it doesn't have the awkward 'teens' between ten and twenty which are a pattern all to themselves.

That, you'd think, would be the end of the story, but alas you'd be wrong. Some things just won't change. People have been telling the time in a certain way for generations, and they weren't about to change now, diolch yn fawr iawn.

So, we're left with the interesting situation where we'll still use 'ugain munud wedi' for 'twenty past' on the clock, as well as unarddeg and deuddeg for eleven and twelve.

Not to mention the dates, but then they told me not to mention the dates. You can, of course, get by perfectly well with the decimal system, but what would be the fun in that?

Here are a few interesting old numbers, use them when you want to liven up a conversation in the bank, if you can find one.

Pymtheg - fifteen

Ugain - twenty

Ugain punt, ugain munud wedi

Deugain - forty

Hanner cant - fifty

Trigain - sixty

Pedwar ugain - eighty

YN AND MEWN – IN

We don't have a word for 'a' in Welsh. By default 'cadair' means 'a chair' while 'y gadair' means 'the chair'. You'll notice that the 'y' causes a soft mutation of 'cadair' because it's a feminine noun. 'Y ci' doesn't soften because 'ci' is a masculine noun.

This would be fine and dandy, but it does have a few knock-on effects.

'yn' and 'mewn' spring to mind.

In a nutshell, if you think of 'mewn' as 'in a' or 'in some' you'll be pretty much sorted. We'll then use 'yn' before proper nouns and particular locations.

Dw i'n gweithio mewn bank – I work in a bank.

Dw i'n gweithio ym manc HSBC – I work in the HSBC bank.

Dw i'n ymddiddori mewn hanes – I take an interest in history.

Dw i'n ymddiddori yn hanes y Celtiaid – I'm interested in Celtic history.

IDIOMS - 5

Dros Ben Llestri

Over the top (of the dishes). I imagine a sink after the Sunday roast, full of dishes to be washed. The window behind them is open; I launch myself into the air and successfully jump through the open window. Perhaps that's a bit over the top.

Malu awyr

Malu awyr – grinding air. Imagine a mill, grinding flour. After all the flour has been processed and the mill is still turning it is grinding air. To talk for the sake of talking, to talk nonsense.

'MYND AT' AND 'MYND I'

Mynd at – to go to

Mynd i – to go into

Be careful if you ever ask a child to go to the river, they might take you at your word!

THE LONG AND WINDING ROAD

After a while you'll be itching to practise your Welsh. Ah, but you might find that you can't always say exactly what you want to. What to do, what to do?

It's a minefield.

You have a vague idea of something that you'd like to say. It might be important, or it might be extremely trivial. Now if it's important, life or death important, you'd be advised to use English and suffer the embarrassment.

Otherwise take a look at the following.

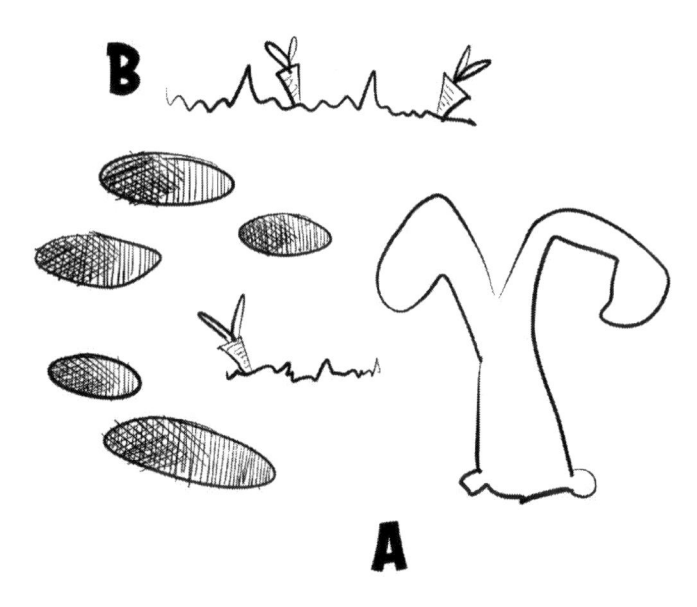

You are at point A and you'd quite like to get to point B through the medium of Welsh. However, you have holes in your Welsh;

gaps in your vocabulary and learning. You could make a run for it and rush in a straight line towards point B, but I'm pretty sure that you'd end up in a hole, no matter how fast you ran.

You could, of course, say nothing. But what'd be the fun in that?

The other option, perhaps the best, is to take a longer, meandering path around the holes.

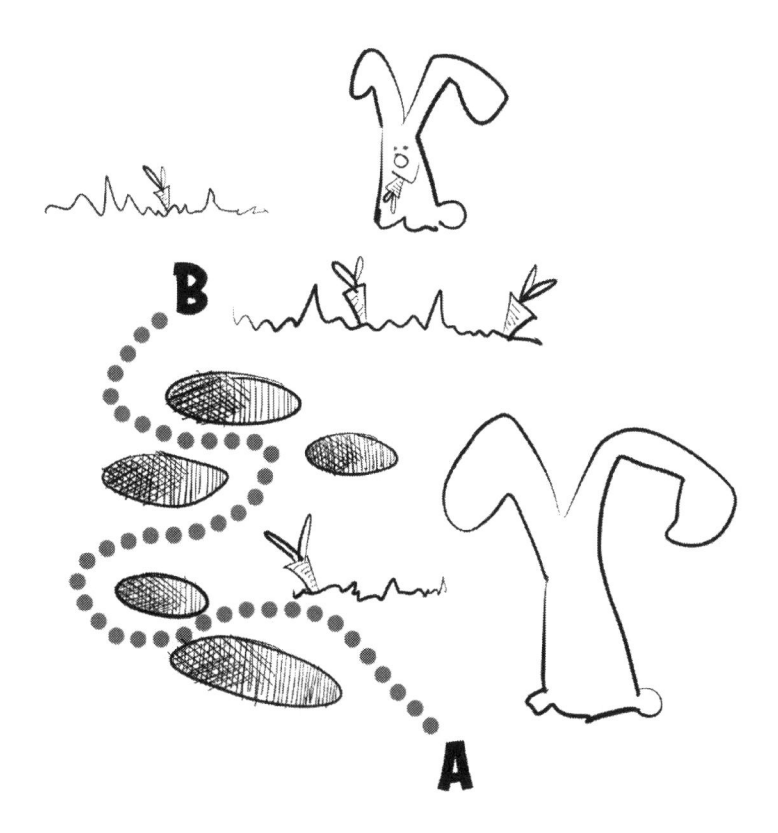

Aralleirio - to say in another way. To paraphrase.

Colin Jones

This will inevitably take longer, as you struggle for words and different tenses, but imagine the pride with which you arrive at your destination! Take your time, look as if you're still talking, and the magic bond of speaking Welsh between two people will remain unbroken.

THE FINAL MUTATION

The aspirate mutation is the third and final mutation, hurray! I've saved it until now as a treat. Actually, I like to call it the antiseptic mutation as the only three letters which can change are T, C and P.

If that wasn't easy enough, the letters that they change to can be found by adding an 'h' to each of them;

T - Th

C - Ch

P - Ph

This mutation doesn't occur that often, but is found after 'ei' meaning 'her' and masculine nouns after 'tri'. It also plays a part at the start of some negative statements too.

Ci - ei chi hi - her dog

Tri chi - three dogs

But;

Tair cath - three cats

Colin Jones

THE SHORT FORM PAST OF BOD

Bues i – I was'd?

Now this is a funny one, if you'll bear with me.

Consider the following;

I was cooking my delicious supper when the phone rang.

However, we wouldn't say - I cooked, when the phone rang.

Ro'n i'n coginio - I was cooking

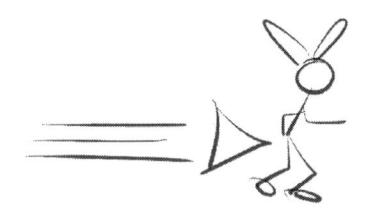

Coginiais i - I cooked

Hopefully the illustrations help show the difference in the ideas. One (I was cooking) takes place throughout a period of time and can be interrupted by something else.

The other is self-contained, and isn't (or wasn't) interrupted.

We're quite happy to jump back and forth between the two tenses in English, and we rarely use the wrong one.

Now let's look at these two tenses using 'to be' in English.

I was walking along when I saw a rabbit.

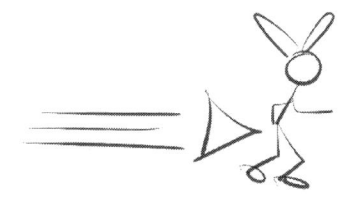

But 'Where were you at the time of the crime?'

I was in the library with Colonel Ketchup and the lead pipe.

The thing is that these two tenses use the same 'I was' in English, but are a little different in Welsh.

Ro'n i'n cerdded - I was walking.

Bues i yn y llyfrgell - I was in the library.

This is by no means a matter of life and death, and you would be best advised to stick with 'ro'n i' until you are completely happy. For now, just recognise the 'bues i' tense when you hear it.

Bues i – I was

Buest ti – you were

Buodd e/hi – He/she was

Buon ni – we were

Buoch chi – you were

Buon nhw – they were

IDIOMS - 6

Gwell crefft na golud

Better a craft than gold. How true, how true. A craft or skill can always be used to make your way in the world. Gold or riches, however, can be spent and with you no more.

Breuddwyd gwrach

A witch's dream. A dream or idea that is unlikely to come to fruition. A pipedream.

Colin Jones

THE SECRET TO LEARNING WELSH

How are the twins?

Oh, the same.

One of my favourite old jokes, but learning Welsh isn't like that. You think you've mastered something, when something new comes along. Some days are good, others not so much. Sometimes you want to give up.

So, what is the secret of learning Welsh? I'm often asked this question, and the answer is always the same; keep at it. You see, and I'm leaving myself open to great potential embarrassment by saying this, I was not very good at learning Welsh when I started.

Yes, I know. Pick yourself up off the floor and close your mouth. Shut the front door. But it's true; for at least the first two years of Welsh classes I had absolutely no idea of what was happening. I remember one particularly perplexing lesson when I had no idea what the tutor was going on about. I looked at the board and could not make any sense out of it. I looked at my book; no idea. Then I looked around, to see the rest of the class happily doing an exercise in their books. It looked pretty bleak at that point. I should have said something, of course, but I was far too shy for that.

For some strange reason I didn't stop at that point. I think I enjoyed the social aspect of classes, and I also picked up some interesting Welsh facts along the way. Did you know that Dewi Sant used to beat himself with twigs while standing in ice-cold rivers, for instance? He was an ascetic monk.

However, not so long afterwards a strange thing began to happen; things started to fall into place. Not as fast as I'd hoped, and certainly not everything, but slowly I began to get a taste for Welsh. Later I did so well that I was asked to tutor classes, but I could have stopped learning that day when things looked bleak. Imagine that. No 'Cadw Swn', no 'Coed y Brenin' and this very book itself would never have existed at all. That's an odd thought.

Most people can learn most languages, unless they stop trying. The longest journey starts with but a single step, and the most pleasurable adventure can often seem off-putting to begin with. You don't need any special talent to learn any particular language, just perseverance. If things look difficult they might well be, or you might be looking at things in the wrong way. Take a break, leave it for now, then see if it makes any sense later on.

Learning Welsh is like learning to drive a car, or learning to knit, or program a computer. It covers a lot of little things, which are not difficult on their own, but take a while to master all together.

There's a saying in Welsh, which sums up this book;

Dyfal donc a dyr y garreg - Repeated taps break the rock

If I can do it, you can too. Dal ati!

Colin Jones

CNOC, CNOC!

Cnoc, Cnoc!

Pwy sy' 'na?

Ceri.

Ceri pwy?

Cer i grafu!

THE CADW SWN GUIDE TO SPEAKING WELSH

'Welsh' is an ugly word; it means foreign. 'Wales' means land of the foreigner. Cymry means 'my people', Cymru 'the land of my people'.

Likewise in Cymraeg 'dysgwr/dysgwraig' refers to someone who is learning Cymraeg. Unfortunately it is often used to describe some-one who has learnt welsh, the term Cymro Cymraeg/Cymraes Cymraeg being reserved for 'Welsh speakers'.

The sooner we ditch these historically misleading terms in both languages the better for all of us. Let's just get on with living and speaking our chosen languages whoever we are, wherever we live.

THE MYTH OF 'DIFFICULT' LANGUAGES

Cymraeg is a straightforward language to learn and speak. I don't joke about these things. If you've come this far, then with a little perseverance and application you will become a perfectly happy and confident speaker of Cymraeg.

You will find many opportunities in your life to speak with other siaradwyr wherever you live.

You will notice the value of the language in your professional and business life.

You will also have another window on the world, with another perspective. Many more books, films and stories to experience; sometimes a clearer picture.

It's certainly worth the effort, and a funny thing seems to happen at this point;

You get more out than you put in.

We can sometimes make things appear difficult, however. Tutors, in particular, seem take a perverse pride in displaying the intricacies of grammar; they think it makes them look good. They might be wrong.

The truth is that if a language, any language, were 'difficult' people just wouldn't speak it. It wouldn't work, it wouldn't hold together. It might be 'different' in some ways, it might make you laugh at its simplicity or frustrated at its apparent complexity, but if it's difficult then you're just not looking at it the right way. (We'll return to this later.)

Anyway, from my perspective, ie an average 'dysgwr', who became an average 'siaradwr' here are a few tips I picked up along the way. If only I knew now what I knew then. (Or should that be the other way around?)

Colin Jones

THE MAGICAL FIRST-LANGUAGE WELSH SPEAKER

We seem to burden 'learners' with an awful number of rules about grammar, mutations, yes/no answers, tenses etc. And yet every year, thousands of children from homes where one or more people speak Cymraeg turn up on their first day of school with a perfectly good command of the language. And do you know what? They haven't had a single grammar lesson! At no point did a well-meaning adult sit them down and explain the nasal mutation or definite articles or diphthongs or the price of fish to them. Why should they?

People speak Cymraeg like any other language; with a 'feel' for how everyone else speaks it. Most of the 'rules' were written after some academic had too much time on their hands one rainy afternoon in Aberystwith. Never ask a speaker of Cymraeg a grammatical question; they'll look at you with a pained expression. They may never speak Cymraeg to you ever again. They are not fountains of the secret knowledge of language, they just happen to speak it!

We can make things difficult by wanting to be correct. We can make things difficult by wanting to know how things work. The truth is that no language works by people learning intricate rules or constructions.

If something is difficult there are two possible explanations:

1. You're looking at it the wrong way. Come back to it later, it'll make more sense.

2. It's difficult. The chances are that most other people think so too. Forget it completely, life's too short.

Colin Jones

IDIOTS GUIDE

I've met a few idiots who speak Cymraeg. Some even mutate in the right places and conjugate their prepositions. They wouldn't know a preposition if you covered it in lard and pushed it through their letterbox. You're obviously not an idiot, but here's a guide anyway:

1. Start a statement with a verb, unless you want to emphasise something.

2. Get your tenses right. God forbid, if necessary learn them! No, really; it works. Get them absolutely right. Every time. There'll be a piece of paper with them all on somewhere. It's in this book, and there's not a huge amount on it. It'll take you two days maximum.

3. Don't bother with Yes and No unless you want to become a gibbering wreck. Just throw in the odd 'Oes' whenever it seems right. Otherwise please use IE and NA. Pretty please.

4. Don't get tied up with mutations. You know how to mutate, but you're not certain when. The simple fact is that if you worry about it you will mutate in the wrong places. Just forget it, and you will naturally speak as everyone else does. Which may not always be 100% correct, by the way.

5. If you don't know how to say something don't. Say something else. Or nothing. Because the moment you

turn to English the spell is broken. They just won't speak to you in Cymraeg again. That's how their minds work.

6. Obviously, if you don't know the word for something use the English, but don't say 'I can't say this in Welsh so I'll say it in English.' Unless you're a doctor, or are talking to one.

THE SECRET TO SIARAD CYMRAEG

Which brings us to the magic formula, y Greal Sanctaidd.

The Secret of Speaking Cymraeg is…

…i siarad Cymraeg.

Soon after I became semi-fluent in Cymraeg I made a decision; I decided that I didn't want to be a learner forever. So I decided that I would not speak English to siaradwyr Cymraeg; dim ond yn Gymraeg. It worked for me. There were very many times when I wanted to say something, but I couldn't. That's how it was. I soon picked up any vocabulary I needed, and they spoke only Cymraeg to me without thinking. And have done ever since.

Just by making that one decision, and that by realising that there was nothing life-threateningly important that I wanted to say, I stopped being a learner.

You might also like to try that with other dysgwyr, it's all you need to do, really.

CNOC, CNOC!

Cnoc, Cnoc!

Pwy sy' 'na?

Ann.

Ann pwy?

Anobeithiol

Cnoc, cnoc.

Pwy sy' 'na?

Dan.

Dan pwy?

Dan ddylanwad.

CEFIN GWLAD YN CYFLWYNO

Y GANTORES ENWOG

MAGGIE CLUST

NOS IAU 31 MEDI 1959

NEUADD Y PENTREF PEN TOST UCHAF

TOCYNNAU 3' 6

SEREN WIB, YR ACROBAT ANHYGOEL

CERI WELD, YN SIARAD AM EI THAITH I AMERICA

HARRI ANIN, Y CERDDOR O BATAGONIA

HOLL ELW AT

GLWB MYNYDDA CANTRE'R GWAELOD

Reference - Sentence Starters-1

As you know, most statements in Welsh start with a verb. Once you're happy with these you're well on the way to fluency. Let's start with the long forms, which are all based on *bod*, to be.

Long forms: present tense; am

me	Dw i	Dw i ddim	Ydw i?
you	Rwyt ti	Dwyt ti ddim	Wyt ti?
he	Mae e	Dyw e ddim	Ydy e?
she	Mae hi	Dyw hi ddim	Ydy hi?
Dafydd	Mae Dafydd	Dyw Dafydd ddim	Ydyn ni?
us	Dyn ni	Dyn ni ddim	Ydych chi?
you	Dych chi	Dych chi didm	Ydyn nhw?
them	Maen nhw	Dyn nhw ddim	

Notice also when 'mae' is used with an indefinite subject (not 'the' or he, she etc);
Mae coffi yn y cwpan.   There is coffee in the cup.
The question is
Oes coffi yn y cwpan?   Is there coffee in the cup?
and the negative is
Does dim coffi yn y cwpan.   There's no coffee in the cup.

Long forms: past tense; was

me	Ro'n i	Do'n i ddim	O'n i?
you	Ro't ti	Do't ti ddim	O't ti?
he	Roedd e	Doedd e ddim	Oedd e?
she	Roedd hi	Doedd hi ddim	Oedd hi?
us	Ro'n ni	Do'n ni ddim	O'n ni?
you	Ro'ch chi	Do'ch chi ddim	O'ch chi?
them	Ro'n nhw	Do'n nhw ddim	O'n nhw?

Long forms: future; will

me	Bydda i	Fydda i ddim	Fydda i ?
you	Byddi di	Fyddi di ddim	Fyddi di?
he	Bydd e	Fydd e ddim	Fydd e?
she	Bydd hi	Fydd hi ddim	Fydd hi?
us	Byddwn ni	Fyddwn ni ddim	Fyddwn ni?
you	Byddwch chi	Fyddwch chi ddim	Fyddwch chi?
them	Byddan nhw	Fyddan nhw ddim	Fyddan nhw?

Long forms: conditional; would

me	Byddwn i	Fyddwn i ddim	Fyddwn i?
you	Byddet ti	Fyddet ti ddim	Fyddet ti?
he	Byddai fe	Fyddai fe ddim	Fyddai fe?
she	Byddai hi	Fyddai hi ddim	Fyddai hi?
us	Bydden ni	Fydden ni ddim	Fydden ni?
you	Byddech chi	Fyddech chi ddim	Fyddech ch?
them	Bydden nhw	Fydden nhw ddim	Fydden nhw?

Reference - Sentence Starters-2

Short Forms: past; did, regular

me	CerddAIS I	CHerddAIS I DDIM	GerddAIS I?
you	CerddAIST TI	CHerddAIST TI DDIM	GerddAIST TI?
he	CerddODD E	CHerddODD E DDIM	GerddODD E?
she	CerddODD HI	CHerddODD HI DDIM	GerddODD HI?
us	CerddON NI	CHerddON NI DDIM	GerddON NI?
you	CerddOCH CHI	CHerddOCH CHI DDIM	GerddOCH CHI?
them	CerddON NHW	CHerddON NHW DDIM	GerddON NHW?

me	BwytAIS I	FwytAIS I DDIM	FwytAIS I?
you	BwytAIST TI	FwytAIST TI DDIM	FwytAIST TI?
he	BwytODD E	FwytODD E DDIM	FwytODD E?
she	BwytODD HI	FwytODD HI DDIM	FwytODD HI?
us	BwytON NI	FwytON NI DDIM	FwytON NI?
you	BwytOCH CHI	FwytOCH CHI DDIM	FwytOCH CHI?
them	BwytON NHW	FwytON NHW DDIM	FwytON NHW?

Did: Mynd, Dod, Gwneud

me	Es i	Es i DDIM	Es i?
you	Est ti	Est ti DDIM	Est ti?
he	Aeth e	Aeth e DDIM	Aeth e?
she	Aeth hi	Aeth hi DDIM	Aeth hi?
us	Aethon ni	Aethon ni DDIM	Aethon ni?
you	Aethoch chi	Aethoch chi DDIM	Aethoch chi?
them	Aethon nhw	Aethon nhw DDIM	Aethon nhw?

Des i	Ddes i DDIM	Ddes i?

Gwnes i	Wnes i DDIM	Wnes i?

Did: Cael

me	Ces i	Ches i ddim	Ges i?
you	Cest ti	Chest ti ddim	Gest ti?
he	Cafodd e	Chafodd e ddim	Gafodd e?
she	Cafodd hi	Chafodd hi ddim	Gafodd hi?
us	Cawson ni	Chawson ni ddim	Gawson ni?
you	Cawsoch chi	Chawsoch chi ddim	Gawsoch chi?
them	Cawson nhw	Chawson nhw ddim	Gawson nhw?

Short Forms: conditional; should

me	Dylwn i	Ddylwn i ddim	Ddylwn i?
you	Dylet ti	Ddylet ti ddim	Ddylet ti?
he	Dylai fe	Ddylai fe ddim	Ddylai fe?
she	Dylai hi	Ddylai hi ddim	Ddylai hi?
us	Dylen ni	Ddylen ni ddim	Ddylen ni?
you	Dylech chi	Ddylech chi ddim	Ddylech ch?
them	Dylen nhw	Ddylen nhw ddim	Ddylen nhw?

Short Forms: conditional; hoffi, would like

Hoffwn i	Hoffwn i ddim	Hoffwn i?

Also available from Cadw Sŵn

The Cadw Sŵn Home-Study Welsh Course

Comprising a printed course book, together with 20 lessons of audio recordings, Cadw Sŵn is a complete home-study Welsh course. Suitable for beginners, or as a revision aid, the course uses stories and classical music to ease and speed your learning. Each lesson has a story, printed in Welsh and English so you always have all the vocabulary to hand. Classical music helps relax and ease the story into your memory.

It took me years to write and perfect, and it'd be the way I'd choose to learn Welsh if I needed to.

Available from www.cadwswn.com

Simple Welsh in an Hour of Your Time

This is a really short book, which gives you the basics of Welsh in an effective and efficient way, taking as short a time as possible. You can use it if you're a complete beginner, or as a revision aid if you're already on the road to fluency. Or maybe if you just find yourself in a rut, and would like a bit of help moving on. Available worldwide on amazon as a printed paperback or Kindle ebook.

The idea is simple; by spending around an hour on this book, with breaks in between chapters, you should be able to master a very simple form of Welsh. A simple form that will let you say what you, or anyone else, is doing, has done, or is going to do, including the negative and question forms.

Coed y Brenin – A Novel for Welsh Learners

Croeso i Aberarthur, pentref bach cysglyd yn y De.

Mae llawer o bobl yn byw yma, ac mae stori gyda phob un. Credwch chi fi.

Welcome to Aberarthur, a small sleepy village in the South.

Lots of people live here, and each has a story. Believe you me.

Apparently Aberarthur is a fictional village, in that it exists only in my mind. The funny thing is that as you read this book it will exist in your mind too, but entirely through the medium of Welsh.

Cwm Gwrachod – A Novel for Welsh Learners

Written by the author of the bestselling Welsh learners' novel Coed y Brenin, this book should help you expand and improve your Welsh, while being both interesting and entertaining.

All our novels are available in paperback, ebook editions or as audio books.

For more details visit www.cadwswn.com

CADWSŴN

Printed in Great Britain
by Amazon